Ellie's Code

Instructional Guide

by Eliana Villarroel

illustrated by Mauricio Sanchez-Patzy

Text and illustrations copyright © 2009 Villarroel

All rights reserved. No part of this book may be reproduced or utilized in any form or by any means, electronic or mechanical, including photocopying, recording, or by any information storage or retrieval system without written permission from the author, except for pages 15, 17, 18, 57, 58, 61 and 62 which may be copied for student practice and record keeping.

Limitation of copyright claim and material excluded from this claim:
Dolch List of High Frequency words.

ISBN 978-0-9911507-1-7

♥

I dedicate my work to the loving memory of my parents,
Carlos Villarroel Soriano & Nelly Blatch-Villarroel.
I also dedicate *Ellie's Code* to all my Special Education students
who embraced the challenge to believe in themselves,
conquered their fears, and realized their dreams
to become fluent readers and good spellers.
They inspired me to seek a different way to teach.
I learned from their mistakes.

♥

Testimonials and Endorsements for *Ellie's Code*

It has been said that teaching reading is rocket science. Indeed, it takes a skilled professional to unlock the mysteries of the written word for many students. While most children learn to read using the standard phonetic approach to reading, there are those for whom this instructional approach does not work. *Ellie's Code* has taken an eclectic approach to teaching reading. Rooted in brain research, *Ellie's Code* is a systematic, sequential, and cumulative reading program which has had a tremendous impact on many of our struggling readers. Some of the students who have found success using *Ellie's Code* have become some of our best readers and writers! I have witnessed a transformation not only in students' reading abilities, but their attitude towards learning as well.

As a principal, I have encouraged many of our teachers to use *Ellie's Code* with their struggling readers as well as their entire class. Many of my teachers have experienced higher levels of reading fluency among their students by using this system. I recommend this program for any student who has not found success through the traditional approach to reading.
T. Alonzo, Ed.D., Principal

Ms. Eliana Villarroel, trained high school students in *Ellie's Code* to tutor elementary school students in reading and spelling. The high school students quickly grasped the concepts and were able to teach the strategies to struggling readers. The color-coded system in *Ellie's Code* teaches students to identify and recall different word patterns. The color-coding assists students to begin reading words and eventually phases out the need for the color-coded text. Students generalize their acquisition of reading strategies to black print in text.

Each student received two–on-one tutoring from a trained high school student for a 50 minute session four times per week over an eight-week period. Before starting *Ellie's Code*, student fluency ranged from 0-39 wpm. After eight weeks of intervention, it ranged from 9 to 109 wpm with an average fluency growth of 39 words per minute.

Our students experienced tremendous success and progress through the use of *Ellie's Code*.
L. Gallegos, Principal

I have witnessed one student after another undergo dramatic changes in their ability to read and spell. From the first lesson *Ellie's Code* provides students with a practical system based on color-coded predictable patterns. The students improve simultaneously their ability to decode, their fluency, and their spelling. The system targets a population of students who cannot be taught by using conventional methods based on a phonemic approach. The simple method used in *Ellie's* Code engages the brain from a different perspective. It bypasses the need to decode using sound discrimination by providing easy to remember visual spelling patterns which the brain can recognize and retain. The students thrive, literally within hours!
S. Preysler, School Psychologist

Ellie's Code, a program for struggling readers, was implemented at our school site this year. Children rapidly made significant gains in reading fluency and spelling accuracy. By the end of the school year, data showed that students made significant improvement in these areas.

Students were motivated by the "child friendly" format of the program. Many students who participated in this intervention program were being considered for Special Education assessment because of delays in reading. They demonstrated such strong reading growth because of *Ellie's Code,* that assessment is no longer being contemplated.

I encourage others to try this dynamic and effective reading program.
J. Fonseca, School Psychologist

I used this system with some at-risk students. It was very successful. They went from being non-readers to reading at grade level.
M. Parrino, Teacher with 24 years experience

This program is awesome because it lets the students learn based on English language spelling patterns. It is useful and systematic. It makes the students feel confident and successful.
E. Chelin, Educational Assistant

The lessons in this book have been the only ones that have truly helped my English Language Learners learn and recall how to spell and use high frequency words. It is easy to use and a great resource.
R. Reyes, Teacher with 12 years experience

I am truly impressed with this valuable concept Ms. Villarroel has developed. I saw an amazing transformation within 30 minutes! My nine year old grandson, who attends a Special Day Class, was able to read and also take dictation, which he had not been able to accomplish before. He has become self-motivated and picks up *Ellie's Code* to read and study on his own.
L. Rosas, Grandmother

I have used this program for the past two years. I have seen great improvement in the reading and the writing skills of children. As compared to other reading programs which I have used in the past, this program is easier to use and gives far better and quicker results. The children enjoy the lessons and love to read the book over and over. I look forward to continue using this program as a reading intervention aid.
M. Valenzuela, Instructional Assistant with 30 years experience

I recommend *Ellie's Code* for all students, especially English Language Learners. This program has helped my struggling students learn to decode with ease and make great improvements in reading fluency and spelling. This program trains the brain to look for spelling patterns through color-coded high frequency words. It helps students become successful readers as it trains them to look for words within words while making learning and teaching an effective and positive experience.
V. Banuelos, Teacher with 12 years experience

CONTENTS

I	Introduction	2
II	Summary Guide for Color-Code Usage	4
III	Lesson Plan, Suggestions, and Strategies	5
IV	*Ellie's Code* Pre-test and Post-test Score Sheet for the Vocabulary List of High Frequency Words	15
V	Student's Reading Test – List of 132 words for *Ellie's Code* Story	16
VI	Color-coded Spelling Patterns Practice Sheets for *Ellie's Code* Word List – 132 Words	17
VII	Color-coded High Frequency Word Lists for *Ellie's Code* Story – 16 Lists – 132 Words	19
VIII	*Ellie's Code* Color-Coded Story With Word Count	27
IX	Color-coded *Dolch List* – 28 Lists – 220 Words	43
X	*Dolch List* – Pre-test and Post Test Score Sheets	57
XI	*Dolch List* – Student's Reading Test – 220 Words	59
XII	Color-coded Spelling Patterns Practice Sheets for *Dolch List* – 220 Words	61

Introduction

Ellie's Code emerged from a deep desire and dedication to develop a method which would allow many struggling students, special education students, and English language learners to decode with ease, acquire reading fluency, and improve English language spelling.

To teach these students successfully, I first had to recognize and comprehend from each child's perspective why reading and spelling was such a difficult task. I had to analyze all possible reasons for student struggles and mistakes in order to design a reading and spelling method that would remove the obstacles and allow the brain to process these tasks with ease and enjoyment. Just as importantly, I needed to understand why traditional programs which were successful for many other students, simply did not work for these students. According to the 2007 National Assessment of Educational Progress (NAEP), the reading achievement level performance of fourth graders performing below the "basic" level was 33 percent.

I have thirty one years of teaching experience at the elementary level with the last eight working as a resource specialist. During this time, I have tested hundreds of students who were failing in school, despite numerous attempts to teach them. They were referred for complete assessments to determine possible placement in special education. The most commonly expressed concern of teachers and parents was the struggle students experience in regular education because they could not read or write. Some students already had been retained and given remedial services.

I have worked with many young students who have experienced school as a world plagued with feelings of inadequacy and frustration. Years of failure have programmed their beautiful young minds to think that the task of reading and spelling is incomprehensible and unattainable. My quest was to find a solution.

As a result of this experience, I came to realize that my greatest knowledge and sense of accomplishment came from the challenge which my special education students had set before me. The reading, research, trial, error, and endless polishing of the color-coded materials were important. However, learning to think and teach differently, based on the analysis of students' mistakes, was at the heart of my work. Consequently, I have developed a method to make learning comprehensible, successful, and enjoyable for any students who struggle with reading and spelling. This is achieved by making decoding and spelling a simple and predictable process, through specifically designed research-based material and procedures. This method has been used successfully in both general and special education classes.

The motto of *Ellie's Code* is "Find the Power to Believe in Yourself Because Failure is Not an Option!" Teacher enthusiasm cannot be underestimated. Students must know their teacher has no doubt about the positive changes they can achieve.

Prior to starting an activity, especially one as complicated as learning to read and spell, children must consciously visualize themselves succeeding. The subconscious mind will believe what the conscious mind suggests and program the brain accordingly by speaking, thinking, or feeling. The subconscious creates a reality based on those actions.

Negative thoughts and apprehensions interfere with learning. When students believe they can learn, they do learn. Realizing their only choice is to succeed, they are poised for success.

As students experience success one step at a time, their attitude starts to change immediately. We know that success improves self-esteem and a positive self-image makes learning easier. The process is circular: improved self-esteem makes learning easier and more enjoyable, which transfers to success in other academic areas, which further increases positive attitudes.

Teachers must perceive students with reading and spelling difficulties as positive challenges. Think of the analogy of a gemologist who identifies a piece of crystallized carbon as a potentially beautiful diamond or a lapidary who cuts and polishes the carbon to reveal a shiny, sparkling diamond. The focus is to remove all that is obscuring the rough piece of carbon to reveal the shiny gem that has laid captive inside. The gemologist and lapidary never have any doubts that there is a diamond inside the rock. And just as a diamond is a mineral composed of carbon crystallized at extremely high temperature and pressure, struggling students have been under extreme heat and pressure to perform for a very long time. In a similar way, the teacher's job is to perceive students with learning difficulties as "diamonds in the rough." The teacher, like the gemologist, must first identify these students. Then, like the lapidary, the teacher must work methodically with precision, skill, determination, and faith to bring out the radiance students experience through the acquisition of knowledge. The method in *Ellie's Code* engages and self-guides the brain to decode through recognition of details and spelling patterns. They polish their skills so that, like diamonds, they too may shine to their fullest brilliance.

Ellie's Code is based upon three research-based principles:

1. The main function of the brain when engaged in learning is to search, identify, extract, and organize patterns. The brain learns through association to construct new meaning based upon previously learned patterns.

2. Color triggers specific attention and responses affecting the cortex within the brain, as well as, the entire nervous system. Blue, green, and red are the colors specifically chosen for *Ellie's Code* because they correlate to the three types of color-sensitive cone photo receptors located in the fovea centralis. These are found in the center of the macula region of the retina in the human eye. These cones are responsible for maximum visual acuity and perception of detail, which is necessary and important in humans for the process of reading.

3. Approximately 50% of all text children read is composed of 100 high-frequency words.

Color-coded material consisting of high-frequency word lists, a controlled-vocabulary story, spelling patterns practice sheets, and follow-up practice stories reinforce spelling pattern recognition, improve decoding ability, and increase reading fluency.

The success experienced by children is evidence of the practicality and efficacy of this method. Teachers, parents, tutors, and students, I invite you to attain the same success by using "Ellie's Code."

SUMMARY GUIDE FOR COLOR-CODE USAGE:

COLOR CODE:	USE:	SAMPLES:
BLUE LETTER (S)	- Identify whole words or mini-words within word(s) and/or spelling patterns which can be easily decoded in isolation.	as, fast, has, all, call, can, the, them, for, only, just, think, story, together, watch, you, before,
GREEN LETTER (S)	- Complete all the sounds required to decode the word when added to the blue letters and/or the blue and red letters. - May serve to identify the change of nouns from singular to plural. - Regular verb-tense endings: (present progressive, past tense) - Adverb endings as needed.	they, was, about, maybe, words, ants legs, pigs, bricks doing, falling, saying, looked, called luckily, proudly
RED LETTER (S)	- Identify silent letter(s). Important to remember for spelling. - May alert the reader to change the previous vowel(s) sound from a short vowel to a long vowel, or vice versa. - Guides the reader to focus on decoding the blue short/long vowel while ignoring the red vowel for vowel digraphs (two successive letters whose phonetic value is a single sound). - Help to distinguish the correct meaning of a homophone (Two or more words pronounced alike but are different in meaning, derivation or spelling.)	one, why, know, watch, school, answered time, made, like, give, have your, yours, could, please, people, thought, because to, too, two right, write their, there hear, here

Ellie's Code Lesson Plan, Suggestions, and Strategies

Ellie's Code Motto:
*"Find the Power to Believe in Yourself
Because Failure is Not an Option!"*

Objective Standards for Grade 2:
Writing Standard: Spell 128 high frequency words with 100% accuracy
Reading Standard: Read aloud with minimum fluency of 70 words per minute with 90% accuracy and with appropriate intonation and expression

Materials
- *Ellie's Code Instructional Guide Book*:
  - *Ellie's Code* story
  - 16 color-coded spelling pattern word lists (128 high frequency words)
  - 28 color-coded spelling pattern word lists consisting of Dolch List words (220 high frequency words)
  - High frequency words pre/post-test record sheets
  - High frequency words practice sheets
  - High frequency words reading list for student practice
- Supplemental Reading Practice
  - Color-coded adaptations of:
  - **The Old Wolf and the Three Little Pigs** - Level 1 (First and second grade)
  - **The Old Wolf and the Little Red Hen** - Level 2 (Second grade and third grade)
  - **The Old Wolf and Jack and the Beanstalk** - Level 3 (Third grade through fifth grade)
  - **Old Wolf's Search for Pinocchio** – Level 4 (Fifth grade and above)
- Student Materials
  - Individual notebooks for spelling and dictation
  (.7 cm² graph paper recommended)
  - Set of blue, green, and red colored pencils for each student (blue, red and green colored **pencils** recommended for easy erasure when correcting work)

Time
Approximately 45 minutes to one hour per session

Student Prior Knowledge Desired, But Not Required
- All consonant letter names
- All consonant sounds
- All five vowel names
- (It is not necessary to know the difference between short or long vowel sounds at this time.)

♦ Step 1 Instructions
- Pre-test each student for baseline reading and spelling levels using *Ellie's Code List* (132 words); record error patterns
- Stop the test if 5 errors occur in the first 10 words in either the reading or the spelling test.
- Pre-test score is for teacher use only

♦ Step 2 Introduce the program by explaining that:
- Students will become better readers and spellers
- The most important concept for students is to believe in themselves; it is the first step in making their belief become a reality
- Ask students: "Do you believe you can do it?"
- Tell them that from that moment on, they will have to tell their brain that they will be able to read and spell.
- When things get difficult, they can only say, "I need more practice," or "I need help."
- Do not allow students to say, "I can't do it!" or "Reading is too hard!"

♦ Step 3 Overview of the brain:
- How and where the brain usually stores written and spoken language
- Instruct students to touch the area above and slightly behind their left ear (left occipital-temporal area)
- Explain that this area of the brain is important for word recognition, storage, and retrieval during visualization activities

♦ Step 4 Color-Coded Spelling Pattern Recognition
Refer to Ellie's Code Summary Chart for basic understanding of the color-code
- Holding up **Ellie's Code List 1,** ask students to identify the spelling patterns.
- Tell students that the mini-word or spelling pattern *an* is colored blue.

*Vowel trigraphs: three vowels written together make only one vowel sound. Most of these words are French-derived: (Examples: obvious, cautiously, courageously)

- Students read words focusing on the color-code patterns. Students must demonstrate reading fluency before progressing to dictation.

♦ Step 5 Visualization - Introduction
Instruct students to:
- Look at word
- Spell word aloud
- Close eyes
- Spell word orally three more times
- The fourth time: visualize the word and spell with eyes closed, telling your brain to store the word just like a computer

Explain that visualizing a word is a technique to store the word in their brains. When students close their eyes, they are blocking out visual interference which may affect word retrieval. Visualization helps the brain access previously learned words and fine-tune the sounds of each word. It helps the student to understand and process sound-symbol correspondence.

♦ Step 6 Visualization - Practice
When students are unable to decode a word, instruct them to:
- Look at the word
- Spell it aloud
- Close their eyes
- Retrieve the word from storage

Explain that by touching the correct area of one's head and closing the eyes, one can help the brain find where the word is stored in the brain. The teacher demonstrates by gently touching the left occipito-temporal side just above and slightly behind the student's left ear. The teacher does this, two or three times, and soon students do it themselves.

This whole process is done to shut off visual stimuli and focus on **the sound-symbol-**sound of a particular word for storage and for future retrieval of that word. This also allows the brain to focus on the task, match the letter-symbols to the corresponding word, and also fine-tune auditory processing.

You may often notice that children with speech difficulties are able to pronounce words more accurately when they hear them and repeat them while their eyes are closed.

Do not try to teach isolated sounds. Let students hear the entire word.

If student cannot retrieve the word, the teacher:
- Whispers the word while the student's eyes are closed (alternate tones)
- Spells the word aloud slowly while the student's eyes are closed
- Asks student to repeat the word with his/her eyes closed.
- Prompts the student by saying:
  "Tell your brain to store the word just like a computer."
- Instruct student to write each word seven times in columns using graph paper and the corresponding colored pencils
- Each word must be written in its entirety switching the corresponding colored pencils; doing otherwise will impede learning

♦ Step 7 Quiz
Administer quiz after students practice all the words on
Ellie's Code List 1 and List 2
- Students use black pencils and graph paper for the quiz and dictation
- Mastery is achieved with:
    Spelling: 100%
    Reading Fluency: 70+ words per minute
    (reading first and second page of controlled-vocabulary story)

♦ Step 8 Correcting the Quiz
Students self-correct the quiz first
To correct errors:
- Tell student which letters are correct
- Point to the incorrect letters
- Ask student what letter(s) should be substituted for the incorrect letter(s)
- If student does not know, instruct student to:

- Close eyes
- Touch left side of temple to visualize
- Listen to the word with his/her eyes closed
- Access the correct spelling to determine which letter(s) to substitute
- If student is unable to access the word or make the correction(s), prompt the student by suggesting a similar word that has the same mini-word or base-word
- Assist students to self-correct the words as often as necessary

♦ Step 9 Additional Practice

- Write each misspelled word correctly seven times using graph paper and three colored pencils to duplicate the color code pattern (see *Ellie's Code List 1* or *2* for the correct color code)
- Reinforce each student as accuracy improves, eventually reaching 100% on each lesson. As student self-esteem increases, so does student effort. Verbally acknowledge student effort and accomplishment as he/she completes each task.
- To reinforce student progress, always record the number correct (e.g. +10) rather than the number wrong (e.g. -2)
- After student masters reading and spelling two word lists, begin reading *Ellie's Code* story
  - Teacher models by reading one page at a time
  - Students read the page orally together
  - Teach each underlined word separately because they are not on the high-frequency word lists
- Oral reading fluency must be mastered before starting dictation activities.
- Minimum fluency is 60-70 wpm reading two pages of *Ellie's Code.*
- Teacher patience is required. At first the work will appear slow and tedious, but the pace quickens as students' brains learn the patterns and techniques. Students progress much faster usually after the third lesson.

♦ Step 10 Dictation

Dictate sentences from each page of the story
- If dictation takes too long, dictate half a page
- **Very important:** *use only graph paper* when doing color-coded practice and dictation
- Graph paper aids students to recognize patterns, count letters, and maintain spacing by leaving one square between each word, one square between each line, and to indent five spaces for each new paragraph

♦ Step 11 Punctuation and Capitalization
- Punctuation and capitalization are taught at the same time, although neither is the main focus of instruction
- At the start of each sentence, prompt students to remember what type of letter to use ("capital" or "upper case")
- During dictation, prompt students to write the correct punctuation mark (period, comma, exclamation mark, question mark, and quotation marks)
- Ask which punctuation mark to use if the speaker is asking a question, shouting or excited, making a statement, naming more than two things, animals, or people, or about to say something
- When finished writing, students read aloud what they have written.
- Teacher and student correct the work together
- Always allow or prompt the student to practice self-correction and editing before offering to help

♦ Step 12 Optional Practice Prior to Administering Post-Test
(use only when additional practice is needed)
- Color-coded dash lines correspond to the words in the test lists
- Color-coded lines prompt students to remember the spelling pattern, location of silent letters, and number of letters in each word
- Students use black lead pencils to write dictation

♦ Step 13 Post-Test
When finished with the sixteen *First High Frequency Word List* lessons, reading the entire story, and the complete dictation of *Ellie's Code*:
- Administer the post-test consisting of all the words arranged in random order
- Students write using only black pencils
- Correct the post-test
- Re-teach only the misspelled words

♦ Step 14 Follow Up
Students listen, read, practice, and take dictation using *The Three Little Pigs* adaptation.
- Teach the color-coded *Dolch Word List* using the same method as above for *Ellie's Code Word List*
- The *Second High Frequency Word Lists* consist of the complete Dolch Word List (120 previously learned words with the addition of the remaining 100 words)

Suggestions
- Prior to practice, ask students to follow along as you read the story. You may have to read one paragraph or one page at a time and then ask students to read back to you. Ask students to pay attention to the intonation and expression of the reader.

- Do not correct errors
  - always allow students to self-correct first
  - if error occurs again, ask the student to:
    - first decode the letters in blue or the mini-word
    - remember that red letters are silent
    - look at the beginning, middle, or ending, of the word to search for a known word
    - when students come to a word which they do not instantly recognize, it is not necessary to decode from left to right - it is better to *first* identify parts of the word which they recognize and *then* read the word from left to right
- After they become fluent readers with *The Old Wolf and the Three Little Pigs*, have students listen to the story about *The Old Wolf and the Little Red Hen*.
- Let them enjoy reading and discussing the story first. Then focus on accuracy.
- Next have students listen and read *The Old Wolf and Jack and the Beanstalk*.
- Let them enjoy reading and discussing the story first. Then focus on practice and accuracy.
- For students in the sixth grade or higher, have them listen and read *Old Wolf's Search for Pinocchio*. Discuss the story and new vocabulary.

Strategies
The following strategies are specific to teaching common homonyms (words with the same sound, different spelling, and different meaning). Children usually have difficulty spelling homonyms.
- **there** and **their**
  - Cover the <u>t</u> in **there**
  - Ask student to read the word that is left: **here**.
  - Tell student the word ***there*** is usually used when referring to location in the same way **here** is used to indicate location
  - Say the sentence "Walk from **here** to ***there***." to illustrate the difference
  - Both words describe location and differ by only one letter.
  - Emphasize that the final letter in ***there*** is a silent <u>e</u>.

- Next examine *their*
    - Cover the **t** leaving the word *heir.*
    - Discuss the meaning of *heir*:
    - One who inherits property, titles, or rank
    - Associate the word *their* with ownership
- Use both words in several sentences, asking students to identify whether the word implies location or possession.

Examples:
   Place your backpack over <u>there</u> by the door.
   Your paper is <u>there</u> on you desk.
   The twins walked to **<u>their</u>** house alone.
   It was **<u>their</u>** idea to wash the dog.

- Ask students to spell the word based upon its meaning
- Remind students that both words begin with the letters **<u>the</u>**: they only have to remember the last two letters (<u>the</u>**re** and <u>the</u>**ir**)

- *to, too,* and *two*
    - Teach *too* by stating that it means **also or very**
        - Ask if anyone likes pizza.
        - Draw an **o** and turn it into a happy face; say, "That is you!"
        - Then put your head next to the happy face and say, "Me, too! I also like pizza."
        - Draw a second face next to the first one (<u>oo</u>)
        - Write the letter **t** in front of the two **o** letters (**<u>too</u>**)
        - Tell students to look at both happy faces and associate them with the two **o** letters because two people happen to like pizza
        - The word **<u>too</u>** means **also** or **very**
- Use all three words in several sentences, asking students to hold up the correct word card signaling <u>to</u>, <u>two</u>, or <u>too</u>.

Examples:
   We went <u>to</u> the park (store, movie, beach, etc).
   I have <u>two</u> hands (eyes, feet, knees, etc.).
   My little brother said, "Me, <u>too</u>," when he heard we were going to the park.
   After mom asked my sister if she wanted a popsicle, I said, "Me, <u>too</u>!"

- Teach **regular past tense** after students learn the word **called** from *Ellie's Code List 2*
    - Identify the **<u>ed</u>** ending as **"Mr. ed"**

- **Mr. ed** does not use a capital letter for his name, but helps us by indicating regular past tense
- **Mr. ed** attaches himself to the end of a present tense verb

- Explain that although the ending is spelled **ed**, it makes three different sounds depending on the **letter sound it follows**:
    - **ed** says /ed/ when following the sound /t/ or /d/
    - **ed** says /t/ when following the sound /f/ (include –**gh**) /k/ /p/ /s/ /sh/ and /ch/
    - **ed** says /d/ when following the sound /b/ /g/ /dg/ /l/ /m/ /n/ /r/ /v/ /z/ /j/

(Note: some consonants are doubled as in *sto**pp**ed* and *gra**bb**ed*)

- When the word ends in **e**, only **d** is added (example: *bake = bake**d***)

- Students should not be expected to memorize these rules
- Tell students the spelling of regular past tense **ed** remains the same regardless of how it is pronounced (/t/ /d/ or /ed/)
One exception exists:
    ·when a word ends in **y**, the **y** changes to **i** and **ed** is added
    (example: *stud**y** = stud**ied***)

- What should be remembered is that the **spelling of regular past tense** remains the same, even when the pronunciation of the final -**ed** is different.

♦ **Step 15** Reading Practice to Improve Reading Fluency
- Depending on the student's grade level, have students read ***The Old Wolf and The Little Red Hen, Old Wolf and Jack and the Beanstalk, and Old Wolf's Search for Pinocchio***
- You read one paragraph at a time
- Have students follow along
- Discuss the meaning of any difficult words
- Have each student re-read the same paragraph you read until the whole story is read.
- Focus on enjoyment, fluency, accuracy, expression, prediction, and comprehension.

Students should be able to read third grade level material by the time they finish reading *The Old Wolf and Jack and the Beanstalk*.

Students should be able to read at least sixth grade level material by the time they finish reading *Old Wolf's Search for Pinocchio*.

Students do not become dependent on *Ellie's Color-Code* to read. They can transition and read all black-letter written material easily. **Do not expect students to remember the color-code.** It is used only as a training strategy to help their brains acquire decoding skill, reading fluency, and spelling accuracy with ease and self-guidance.

I know you and your students will be very pleased with the results.

Vocabulary List for *Ellie's Code* - Pre-test and Post-test

Reading Score /132 - Spelling Score /132   Date:

#	Word	READ	SPELL	#	Word	READ	SPELL	#	Word	READ	SPELL
1	a			34	an			67	and		
2	than			35	many			68	want		
3	that			36	what			69	water *		
4	was			37	has			70	ask		
5	had			38	all			71	call		
6	small			39	he			72	her		
7	she			40	we			73	were		
8	been			41	green			74	see		
9	get			42	the			75	then		
10	they			43	these			76	other		
11	their			44	those			77	I		
12	his			45	this			78	wish		
13	big			46	if			79	of		
14	it			47	its			80	again		
15	in			48	into			81	today		
16	too			49	two			82	or		
17	more			50	words *			83	do		
18	did			51	said			84	so		
19	some			52	from			85	up		
20	on			53	only			86	long		
21	no			54	not			87	look		
22	go			55	over			88	after		
23	where			56	pretty			89	very		
24	by			57	my			90	way		
25	may			58	say			91	made		
26	have			59	gave			92	are		
27	time *			60	little			93	people		
28	us			61	must			94	just		
29	first			62	most			95	would		
30	you			63	your			96	yours		
31	about			64	with			97	will		
32	which			65	each			98	read		
33	now			66	how			99	own		
100	can										
101	at										
102	as										
103	please										
104	called *										
105	help										
106	be										
107	keep										
108	them										
109	there										
110	is										
111	him										
112	off										
113	find										
114	to										
115	for										
116	does										
117	soon										
118	but										
119	one										
120	good										
121	when										
122	try										
123	away										
124	make										
125	like										
126	use										
127	jump										
128	could										
129	out										
130	who										
131	know										
132	down										

Ellie's Code High Frequency Words for the Student's Reading/Spelling Test

1	a	34	an	67	and	100	can
2	than	35	many	68	want	101	at
3	that	36	what	69	water *	102	as
4	was	37	has	70	ask	103	please
5	had	38	all	71	call	104	called *
6	small	39	he	72	her	105	help
7	she	40	we	73	were	106	be
8	been	41	green	74	see	107	keep
9	get	42	the	75	then	108	them
10	they	43	these	76	other	109	there
11	their	44	those	77	I	110	is
12	his	45	this	78	wish	111	him
13	big	46	if	79	of	112	off
14	it	47	its	80	again	113	find
15	in	48	into	81	today	114	to
16	too	49	two	82	or	115	for
17	more	50	words *	83	do	116	does
18	did	51	said	84	so	117	soon
19	some	52	from	85	up	118	but
20	on	53	only	86	long	119	one
21	no	54	not	87	look	120	good
22	go	55	over	88	after	121	when
23	where	56	pretty	89	very	122	try
24	by	57	my	90	way	123	away
25	may	58	say	91	made	124	make
26	have	59	gave	92	are	125	like
27	time *	60	little	93	people	126	use
28	us	61	must	94	just	127	jump
29	first	62	most	95	would	128	could
30	you	63	your	96	yours	129	out
31	about	64	with	97	will	130	who
32	which	65	each	98	read	131	know
33	now	66	how	99	own	132	down

Practice Test for Ellie's Code High Frequency Words - Page 1

Name:_____ Date:_____ Score:_____ /132

1 __ _	21 __ __	41 __ __ __ __	61 __ __ __
2 __ __ __	22 __ __	42 __ __ __	62 __ __ __ __
3 __ __ __	23 __ __ __ __	43 __ __ __ __	63 __ __ __ __
4 __ __	24 __ __	44 __ __ __	64 __ __ __ __
5 __ __	25 __ __ __	45 __ __ __	65 __ __ __ __
6 __ __ __	26 __ __ __ __	46 __ __	66 __ __ __ __
7 __ __ __	27 __ __	47 __ __	67 __ __ __
8 __ __ __	28 __ __	48 __ __ __	68 __ __ __ __
9 __ __	29 __ __ __ __	49 __ __ __	69 __ __ __ __
10 __ __ __	30 __ __ __	50 __ __ __	70 __ __ __
11 __ __ __ __	31 __ __ __ __	51 __ __ __	71 __ __ __ __
12 __ __ __	32 __ __ __ __	52 __ __ __ __	72 __ __ __
13 __ __	33 __ __ __	53 __ __ __	73 __ __ __ __
14 __ __	34 __ __	54 __ __	74 __ __ __
15 __ __	35 __ __ __ __	55 __ __ __ __	75 __ __ __ __
16 __ __ __	36 __ __ __ __	56 __ __ __ __ __	76 __ __ __ __
17 __ __ __	37 __ __	57 __ __	77 __
18 __ __ __	38 __ __ __	58 __ __ __	78 __ __ __ __
19 __ __ __	39 __ __	59 __ __ __ __	79 __ __
20 __ __	40 __ __	60 __ __ __ __ __	80 __ __ __ __

Practice Test for Ellie's Code High Frequency Words - Page 2

Name:_____ Date:_____ Score: _____ /132

81 __ __ __ __	101 __ __	121 __ __ __
82 __ __	102 __ __	122 __ __ __
83 __ __	103 __ __ __ __	123 __ __ __
84 __ __	104 __ __ __ __	124 __ __ __
85 __ __	105 __ __ __	125 __ __ __
86 __ __ __	106 __ __	126 __ __ __
87 __ __ __	107 __ __ __	127 __ __ __
88 __ __ __ __	108 __ __ __	128 __ __ __ __
89 __ __ __	109 __ __ __ __	129 __ __ __
90 __ __	110 __ __	130 __ __
91 __ __ __	111 __ __ __	131 __ __ __
92 __ __	112 __ __	132 __ __ __
93 __ __ __ __	113 __ __ __	
94 __ __ __	114 __ __	
95 __ __ __ __	115 __ __ __	
96 __ __ __ __	116 __ __ __	
97 __ __ __	117 __ __ __	
98 __ __ __	118 __ __ __	
99 __ __	119 __ __ __	
100 __ __ __	120 __ __ __	

Ellie's Code High Frequency Word Lists

List 1

a
an
and
can
*than
many
want
at
that
what
**water

List 2

as
was
has
ask
please
had
all
call
*called
small

All words marked with two ** are **not** considered high frequency words.
All words with one * were found in Fry's Sight Words, but were not on the Dolch List.
All other high frequency words derived from the Dolch List.

Ellie's Code High Frequency Word Lists

List 3	List 4
she	the
he	then
her	them
help	they
get	these
we	*other
were	there
be	their
been	those
green	
see	
keep	

All words marked with two ** are **not** considered high frequency words.
All words with one * were found in Fry's Sight Words, but were not on the Dolch List.
All other high frequency words derived from the Dolch List.

Ellie's Code High Frequency Word Lists

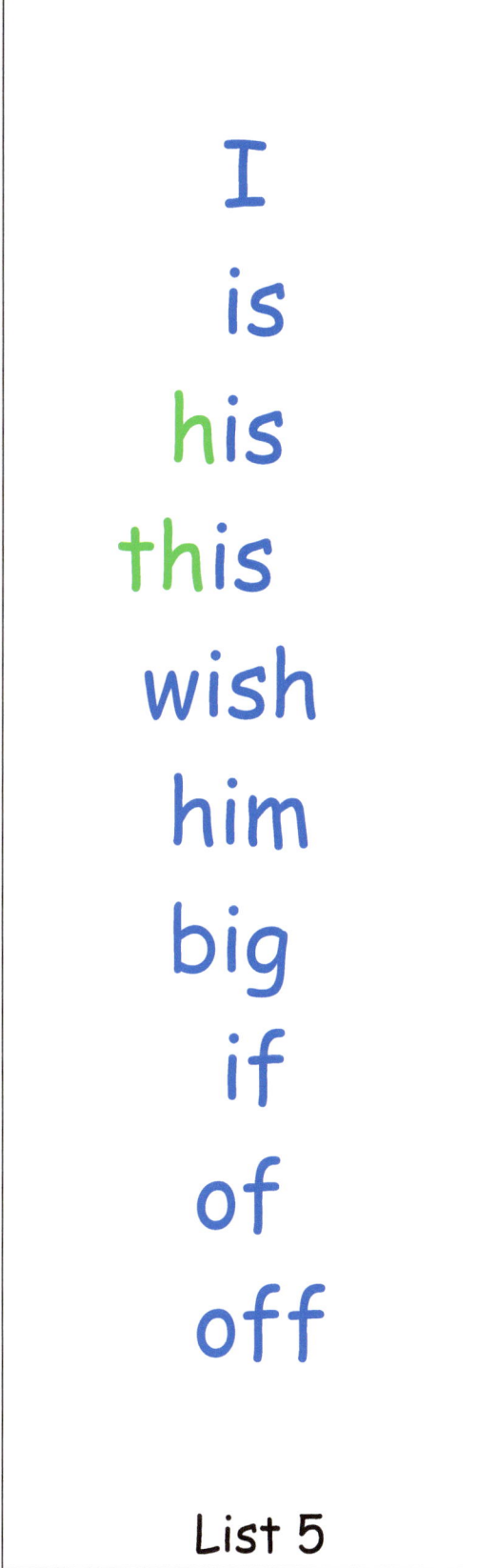

I
is
his
this
wish
him
big
if
of
off

List 5

it
its
again
find
in
into
today
to
too
two

List 6

All words marked with two ** are **not** considered high frequency words.
All words with one * were found in Fry's Sight Words, but were not on the Dolch List.
All other high frequency words derived from the Dolch List.

Ellie's Code High Frequency Word Lists

or
for
*more
**words
do
does
did
said

List 7

so
soon
some
from
up
but

List 8

All words marked with two ** are **not** considered high frequency words.
All words with one * were found in Fry's Sight Words, but were not on the Dolch List.
All other high frequency words ferived from the Dolch List.

Ellie's Code High Frequency Word Lists

List 9	List 10
on	over
only	after
long	where
one	when
no	
not	
look	
good	
go	

All words marked with two ** are **not** considered high frequency words.
All words with one * were found in Fry's Sight Words, but were not on the Dolch List.
All other high frequency words derived from the Dolch List.

Ellie's Code High Frequency Word Lists

List 11	List 12
pretty	made
very	make
try	have
by	gave
my	are
*way	like
away	**time
may	little
say	*people

All words marked with two ** are **not** considered high frequency words.
All words with one * were found in Fry's Sight Words, but were not on the Dolch List.
All other high frequency words derived from the Dolch List.

Ellie's Code High Frequency Word Lists

List 13	List 14
use	would
us	could
jump	you
just	*your
must	yours
*most	out
first	about

All words marked with two ** are **not** considered high frequency words.
All words with one * were found in Fry's Sight Words, but were not on the Dolch List.
All other high frequency words derived from the Dolch List.

Ellie's Code High Frequency Word Lists

List 15	List 16
with	know
will	now
who	how
which	own
*each	down
read	

All words marked with two ** are **not** considered high frequency words.
All words with one * were found in Fry's Sight Words, but were not on the Dolch List.
All other high frequency words derived from the Dolch List.

Word List 1

a
an
and
can
*than
many
want
at
that
what
**water

A cat has a red hat.	6
That cat is fat.	10
Can all cats be fat?	15
The cat called the rat.	20
The cat is <u>bigger</u> than the rat.	27
The rat is bigger than the ants.	34

Word List 2

as

was

has

ask

please

had

all

call

*called

small

That ant was almost as tall as the other ant. 10

The ants were looking at the rat. 17

What are the rat and the cat doing? 25

The rat can see an ant in the water. 34

She had to call the cat. 40

Word List 3

she

he

her

help

get

we

were

be

been

see

green

keep

The ants can see the cat. 6

He has his big, red hat. 12

The ants can call the rat and the cat. 21

They called them to ask how they had been. 30

The ants had their fans. 35

These fans are made of plants. 41

Word List 4

the
then
them
they
these
*other
there
their
those

They sat on their fans.

Their fans are green.

The rat wanted to see the cat.

She went there to see the fat cat.

Then, she was happy to see those ants.

She gave them some food and asked them,

"What do you want to be if you could be someone else?"

Word List 5

I

is

his

this

wish

him

big

if

of

off

"Today we are happy just to be ants!" answered the ants. 11

Then, the rat called the cat saying, "This call is from the 23 rat. Tell the cat that I just found his two friends, the ants. 36 I am calling to ask him if he knew that they had run off 50 to play by the water." 55

Just then, the rat went to look for the cat. By now 67 she was hungry and thought, "I can see two ants on his 79 plants! How I wish these ants were made of candy!" 89

31

Word List 6

it

its

again

find

in

into

today

to

too

two

Later, one of the ants fell in the water! It was sad to see her with her eyes shut and falling off her fan. Her fan was sinking into the water.

The other ant went in the water with its fan, too. Now, two ants were in the water! The rat went in the water, too. The ants asked her for help, "Can you please help us find our two fans?"

"Forget the fans! Get on top of my back!" said the rat.

Word List 7

or

for

*more

**words

do

does

did

said

Back on land, one ant said, "I can hear some words far away."

"I can hear them, too!" said the other ant.

"Those are not words! Those are more ants with fans making all that noise! I can see them coming from up here!" the rat said. Then the rat asked, "Do you want to have another fan or did the other ant go up the tree to get a fan, too?"

"She had one or two fans, but they fell into the water and again she went in to get them!" the ant told the rat.

Word List 8

so

soon

some

from

up

but

The rat swam over to look and she saw the small ant in the water. "I told her to be careful, so now what can I do for her? Does she want this fan or that one over there, so she can get on top of it?" asked the rat.

"I have more fans from my sisters," said the ant. The rat gave the two fans to the small ant. "I only want one long fan, not two fans!" said the ant.

Word List 9

on

only

long

one

no

not

look

good

go

Later that day, the cat came by looking for his friends. The rat looked at him and said, "She was here and then she went over there. After that I did not see her anymore. She had the long fan in one hand and the water was going fast! When I looked for her after that, there were other ants over here and over there."

Word List 10

over

after

where

when

The other ants came by and said, "We were looking for them for a long time, but no one knew where they were!"

Just then, the cat was about to step on the small ant. The rat had to shout to the cat, "Watch out! Do not step on her!"

The cat took one look at them and after that he said, "Oh, no!" Then he jumped and took off. Where the cat went, no one will ever know!

Word List 11

pretty

very

try

by

my

*way

away

may

say

At last, the small ants were out of the water and safe. The big ants came by to say "Hi!" The little ant did not know where she was when she saw that there were so many ants by her side.

Pretty soon she got up and ran over to ask them, "May I be your friend? I like to meet big ants. I was on my way to school, but I still have some time to make friends. All of you look just like me!"

Word List 12

made

make

have

gave

are

like

**time

little

*people

"People are coming!" shouted one of the big ants. 9

They all called each other to say, "We must all run 20 away!" This made the ants very scared and they did 30 not know which way to go. 36

Each of the ants dropped its fan and began to run. 47 They ran very fast, but there was no time for all the ants 60 to get away. "We are trying to run as fast as we 72 can!" the little ant said. 77

38

Word List 13

use

us

jump

just

must

*most

first

The first big ant said, "We must use our six legs to run. We must get away as fast as we can. Most of us could hide under the plants."

The other big ant said, "You must get your fans and put them on top of your backs! That way, you will all look like a big plant."

Then all the ants shouted, "We think that would be a good idea, we should do it now!"

Word List 14

would

could

you

*your

yours

out

about

The people came by and the ants hid under their fans. The small ant did not have time to get away and was still hiding under her fan. A man was about to step on her, when all of a sudden, the cat came back. The man turned around to see the cat dancing on two legs on top of his red hat!

"Who is that cat dancing on top of his red hat?" the people asked. Who would have thought that the cat could have such a good plan to make the people turn around and go back?

Word List 15

with

will

who

which

*each

read

In the end, the ant was saved! "How can I thank you, cat, for saving my life?" asked the little ant who was still hiding under her fan.

Then the cat knelt down to shake her hand and replied, "You are welcome! Just be careful the next time you play down by the water! And don't forget to thank the rat! Now you better go. You must get to school on time because today is your spelling test!"

Luckily everyone got to school safe. Then, the rat

41

Word List 16

know

now

how

own

down

said proudly, "Now with all of this, which I am about to tell each one of you, I know that by now you must know how to read and spell all of your words! You learned it by using Ellie's Code! You should be proud because now you know which letters to use to spell so many words! By now you know how to do it on your own! This story and test is yours to keep and read to someone else."

Then the rat waved good-bye to us saying, "Maybe, just maybe, I will see you someday around the playground."

Dolch List - Second High Frequency Word Lists

List 1	List 2
a	as
an	ask
and	was
any	wash
many	has
can	fast
ran	please
thank	read
want	had
clean	
am	

Dolch List - Second High Frequency Word Lists

at
that
what
eat
ate
are
far
warm
start

List 3

all
call
fall
small
shall

List 4

Dolch List - Second High Frequency Word Lists

he she help her where here were we went me	red let get yes well tell ten seven open
List 5	List 6

Dolch List - Second High Frequency Word Lists

see
keep
sleep
green
three
be
been
because

List 7

the
then
them
they
there
their
these
those

List 8

Dolch List - Second High Frequency Word Lists

List 9	List 10
I	in
is	sing
his	bring
this	think
him	drink
big	find
if	kind
it	again
its	
sit	
six	

Dolch List - Second High Frequency Word Lists

on
upon
only
once
one
long
soon
no
not
hot
both

List 11

so
some
or
for
before
work
of
off

List 12

Dolch List - Second High Frequency Word Lists

do	two
does	too
don't	to
done	into
did	together
said	today
	stop
List 13	List 14

Dolch List - Second High Frequency Word Lists

go	up
going	run
goes	but
got	cut
good	put
look	full
old	pull
cold	much
hold	jump
	hurt
List 15	List 16

Dolch List - Second High Frequency Word Lists

buy
by
my
myself
try
fly
why

List 17

play
say
may
away
always
draw
saw

List 18

Dolch List - Second High Frequency Word Lists

very
every
carry
pretty
funny

List 19

like
ride
live
five
give
gave
have

List 20

Dolch List - Second High Frequency Word Lists

List 21	List 22
come	slow
came	yellow
take	grow
make	know
made	now
little	how
white	own
write	brown
	down

Dolch List - Second High Frequency Word Lists

out
about
round
around
found
our
four
from

List 23

you
yours
would
could
walk

List 24

Dolch List - Second High Frequency Word Lists

use
us
just
must
first
best

List 25

will
with
wish
who
when
which

List 26

Dolch List - Second High Frequency Word Lists

over
after
under
better
never
new

List 27

eight
light
right
laugh
pick
black
blue

List 28

Dolch List (HFW List 2) - Pre-test and Post-test Part 1

Name: Date:

Reading Score /220 Spelling Score /220

	Read	Spell		Read	Spell		Read	Spell
1	a		31	an		61	and		91	any	
2	many		32	can		62	ran		92	thank	
3	want		33	clean		63	am		93	as	
4	ask		34	was		64	wash		94	has	
5	fast		35	please		65	read		95	had	
6	at		36	that		66	what		96	eat	
7	ate		37	are		67	far		97	warm	
8	start		38	all		68	call		98	fall	
9	small		39	shall		69	he		99	she	
10	help		40	her		70	where		100	here	
11	were		41	we		71	went		101	me	
12	red		42	let		72	get		102	yes	
13	well		43	tell		73	ten		103	seven	
14	open		44	see		74	keep		104	sleep	
15	green		45	three		75	be		105	been	
16	because		46	the		76	then		106	them	
17	they		47	there		77	their		107	these	
18	those		48	I		78	is		108	his	
19	this		49	him		79	big		109	if	
20	it		50	its		80	sit		110	six	
21	in		51	sing		81	bring		111	think	
22	drink		52	find		82	kind		112	again	
23	on		53	upon		83	only		113	once	
24	one		54	long		84	soon		114	no	
25	not		55	hot		85	both		115	so	
26	some		56	or		86	for		116	before	
27	work		57	of		87	off		117	do	
28	does		58	don't		88	done		118	did	
29	said		59	two		89	too		119	to	
30	into		60	together		90	today		120	stop	

Name: _____

Dolch List (HFW List 2) - Pre-test and Post-test Part 2 - Reading Score /220 - Spelling Score /220

		Read	Spell			Read	Spell			Read	Spell			Read	Spell
121	go			151	going			181	goes			211	got		
122	good			152	look			182	old			212	cold		
123	hold			153	up			183	run			213	but		
124	cut			154	put			184	full			214	pull		
125	much			155	jump			185	hurt			215	buy		
126	by			156	my			186	myself			216	try		
127	fly			157	why			187	play			217	say		
128	may			158	away			188	always			218	draw		
129	saw			159	very			189	every			219	carry		
130	pretty			160	funny			190	like			220	ride		
131	live			161	five			191	give						
132	gave			162	have			192	come						
133	came			163	take			193	make						
134	made			164	little			194	white						
135	write			165	slow			195	yellow						
136	grow			166	know			196	now						
137	how			167	own			197	brown						
138	down			168	out			198	about						
139	round			169	around			199	found						
140	our			170	four			200	from						
141	you			171	yours			201	would						
142	could			172	walk			202	use						
143	us			173	just			203	must						
144	first			174	best			204	will						
145	with			175	wish			205	who						
146	when			176	which			206	over						
147	after			177	under			207	better						
148	never			178	new			208	eight						
149	light			179	right			209	laugh						
150	pick			180	black			210	blue						

Dolch List - 220 High Frequency Words For the Student's Reading/Spelling Test

1	a	31	an	61	and	91	any
2	many	32	can	62	ran	92	thank
3	want	33	clean	63	am	93	as
4	ask	34	was	64	wash	94	has
5	fast	35	please	65	read	95	had
6	at	36	that	66	what	96	eat
7	ate	37	are	67	far	97	warm
8	start	38	all	68	call	98	fall
9	small	39	shall	69	he	99	she
10	help	40	her	70	here	100	where
11	were	41	we	71	went	101	me
12	red	42	let	72	get	102	yes
13	well	43	tell	73	ten	103	seven
14	open	44	see	74	keep	104	sleep
15	green	45	three	75	be	105	been
16	because	46	the	76	then	106	them
17	they	47	there	77	their	107	these
18	I	48	is	78	his	108	this
19	him	49	big	79	if	109	it
20	its	50	sit	80	six	110	in
21	sing	51	bring	81	think	111	drink
22	find	52	kind	82	on	112	again
23	on	53	upon	83	only	113	once
24	one	54	long	84	soon	114	no
25	not	55	hot	85	both	115	so
26	some	56	or	86	for	116	before
27	work	57	of	87	off	117	do
28	does	58	don't	88	done	118	did
29	said	59	two	89	too	119	to
30	into	60	together	90	today	120	stop

Dolch List - 220 High Frequency Words For Student's Reading/Spelling Test

121	go	151	going	181	goes	211	got
122	good	152	look	182	old	212	cold
123	hold	153	up	183	run	213	but
124	cut	154	put	184	full	214	pull
125	much	155	jump	185	hurt	215	buy
126	by	156	my	186	myself	216	try
127	fly	157	why	187	play	217	say
128	may	158	away	188	always	218	draw
129	saw	159	very	189	every	219	carry
130	pretty	160	funny	190	like	220	ride
131	live	161	five	191	give		
132	gave	162	have	192	come		
133	came	163	take	193	make		
134	made	164	little	194	white		
135	write	165	slow	195	yellow		
136	grow	166	know	196	now		
137	how	167	own	197	brown		
138	down	168	out	198	about		
139	round	169	around	199	found		
140	our	170	four	200	from		
141	you	171	yours	201	would		
142	could	172	walk	202	use		
143	us	173	just	203	must		
144	first	174	best	204	will		
145	with	175	wish	205	who		
146	when	176	which	206	over		
147	after	177	under	207	better		
148	never	178	new	208	eight		
149	light	179	right	209	laugh		
150	pick	180	black	210	blue		

Practice Sheet for Color-Coded Spelling Patterns of 220 Word Dolch List

Name:_____ Date:_____ Score_____/220

www.ingramcontent.com/pod-product-compliance
Lightning Source LLC
Chambersburg PA
CBHW040055160426
43192CB00002B/72